little book **BIG** idea

What is money?

NoodleJUICE

Noodle Juice Ltd
www.noodle-juice.com
Stonesfield House, Stanwell Lane, Great Bourton, Oxfordshire, OX17 1QS
First published in Great Britain 2023
Copyright © Noodle Juice Ltd 2023
Text by Noodle Juice 2022 • Illustrations by Katie Rewse 2022

Printed in China
A CIP catalogue record of this book is available from the British Library.
ISBN: 978-1-915613-01-1
10 9 8 7 6 5 4 3 2 1

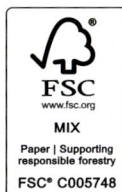

FSC
www.fsc.org
MIX
Paper | Supporting
responsible forestry
FSC® C005748

This book is made from
FSC®-certified paper.
By choosing this book, you
help to take care of the
world's forests.
Learn more: www.fsc.org.

What is money?

Everyone knows about money, right?

People use it to pay for things, such as food or clothing or toys, but what do you REALLY know about it?

Where does money come from?
(page 4)

Who were the first people to use money?
(page 6)

Is money good?
(page 14)

What is money used for?
(page 8)

Is money the same all over the world?
(page 10)

Who looks after our money?
(page 12)

How does money grow?
(page 16)

GREEN GROCER

How do people earn money?
(page 18)

Refill Shop

Reduce
Reuse
Recycle
Refill

What are taxes?
(page 20)

What problems can money cause?
(page 24)

What is the future of money?
(page 26)

Who studies money?
(page 22)

Where does money come from?

Long ago, people traded things they owned, such as wheat or elephants, with each other. This was called **bartering**.

But elephants are **heavy**, difficult to move and wheat can rot.

So people began to trade **spices and jewellery**, which were also valuable, but easier to carry and didn't rot.

Then, people started to use **tokens**, such as shells, to pay for things.

Eventually, people in different towns believed that one shell held the **same value** as another.

Coins made from **precious metals** then replaced shells. The coins were weighed, so everyone knew that they were the same.

Later, **paper money** appeared in China and Europe as an I.O.U. note for coins.

BALANCE £2168

These days, most money is stored **electronically** in people's bank accounts.

Who were the first people to use money?

Almost 5000 years ago, the first people to use metal for money were the Babylonians. Say it like this:

BAB-ee-LOW-nee-uns

They lived in a city called Babylon, which was located in present-day Iraq. The city started as a small port and fishing village and grew into one of the largest trading cities of the ancient world.

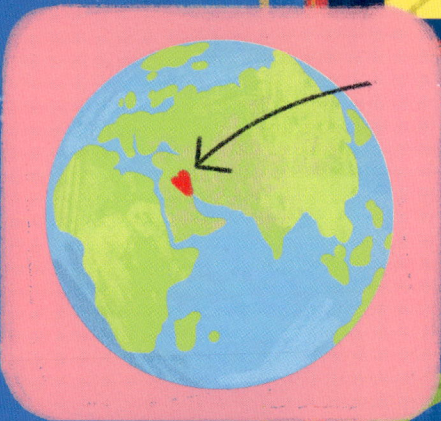

The first person to use **metal coins** was Croesus, King of Lydia. The coins were shaped like beans and made of electrum, a mixture of silver and gold.

What is money used for?

To buy things...

...such as **food** or clothing.

To pay people for the **work they do**.

To pay for somewhere to **live**.

To go on **holiday**.

To buy **presents** or sweets.

To pay for tickets to see a film or a rock concert.

Or a trip to the hairdresser.

Some people **lend** money to others to help them buy a house, or start a business.

BUSINESS LOANS

AVAILABLE

DOG GROOM

Some people **save** their money for the future.

Other people **donate** their money to charity.

Is money the same all over the world?

Each country has their own kind of money. It's called 'currency'.

British pound sterling.

United States dollar.

$

£5

£

Chinese renminbi.

¥

100 YUAN

Japanese yen.

¥

European euro.

1 EURO

10 EURO

€

2000

There are many types of dollar in the world, such as the Korean or New Zealand dollar, but they all have different values.

To work out what your money is worth in another country, you use an exchange rate. This rate can change every day.

One US dollar might be worth seven Chinese renminbi today, but eight tomorrow.

Multiply the amount of your currency by the exchange rate, and you will know how much of the other country's currency you have.

Most countries' governments print paper money and make coins at a factory called a 'mint'.

As more people use electronic banking, it is very easy to transfer any currency all over the world.

Who looks after our money?

Most businesses and people keep their money in banks or building societies. They trust the banks to keep their money safe.

BANK

CASH withdrawals

Governments look after their country's money. They decide how much is spent on education, health and transport.

National banks, such as the Bank of England, help to look after a country's money by setting **interest rates** to manage inflation.

Inflation is when prices for everyday objects such as food or petrol rise at a **faster rate** than the amount of money people earn, leaving them with less to spend.

Banks and building societies use interest rates to work out how **much** money to pay people who keep savings in their bank. Banks then use those savings to make money for themselves.

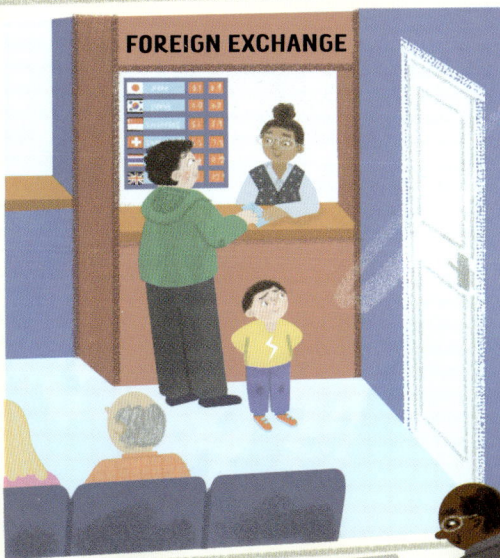

FOREIGN EXCHANGE

It's a good idea to **save** money if you can, in case you need it in the future.

INTEREST FREE 0% 12 months

If you want to borrow money from a bank, they use interest rates to work out how much to **charge** for the loan.

Is money good?

Having enough money means you can buy food and clothing. You have shelter and education. That is a good thing. Some people are lucky enough to have money left over.

A good person with lots of leftover money may decide to help other people. They are called philanthropists.

fi-LAN-THRO-pists

They support **research** into medicine and science.

They provide funds for the **arts** and culture.

Many wealthy people **donate** to charities that help people who have very little or face challenges in life.

However if someone is GREEDY and wants to make lots of money for themselves, they may make decisions that can harm people.

A builder might choose cheaper materials which may not be **safe** because he wants to keep the money saved for himself.

A politician might be influenced by someone's money to make a decision that benefits that person. This is called a **bribe** and is illegal in most countries.

Money isn't good or bad, it's how the people who have money CHOOSE to use it that makes the difference.

How does money grow?

Money may not grow on trees, but it can be encouraged to grow in other ways.

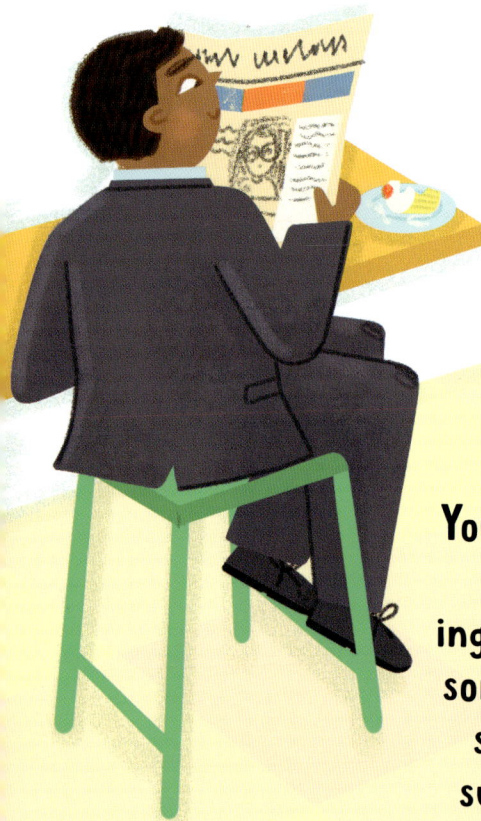

You could use your money to buy ingredients to make something you can sell for **more**, such as cupcakes.

Investing in a **business** that is doing well, such as your bakery, means that your money will grow and you can save.

Interest rates on savings **increases** those savings.

16

You can also make your money work harder for you, so you receive more value for it.

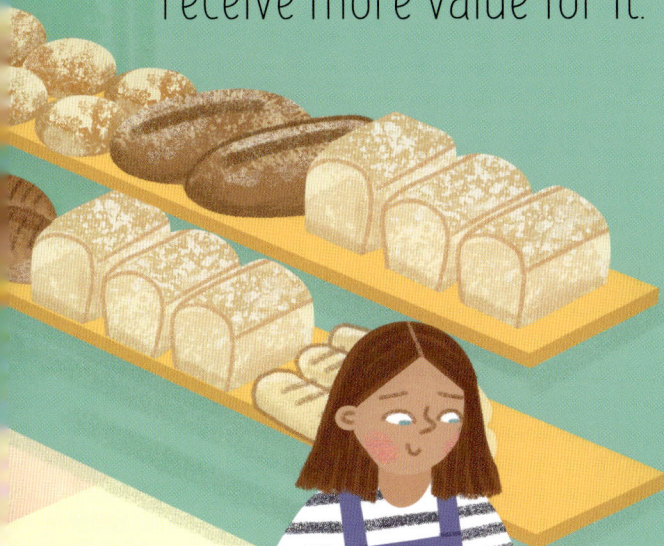

Grouping together to buy things in bulk means you can get a **better** price for ten bags of flour instead of two.

Negotiating or **haggling** over a price can often lead to a lower price. You will have money left over to spend on something else, such as sprinkles for your cupcakes.

How do people earn money?

One way to earn money is to swap your **time and effort** for payment, called wages or a salary.

Some people's time and effort is perceived to be **worth more** than others.

Often, the more **education** you have received, the more money you can earn.

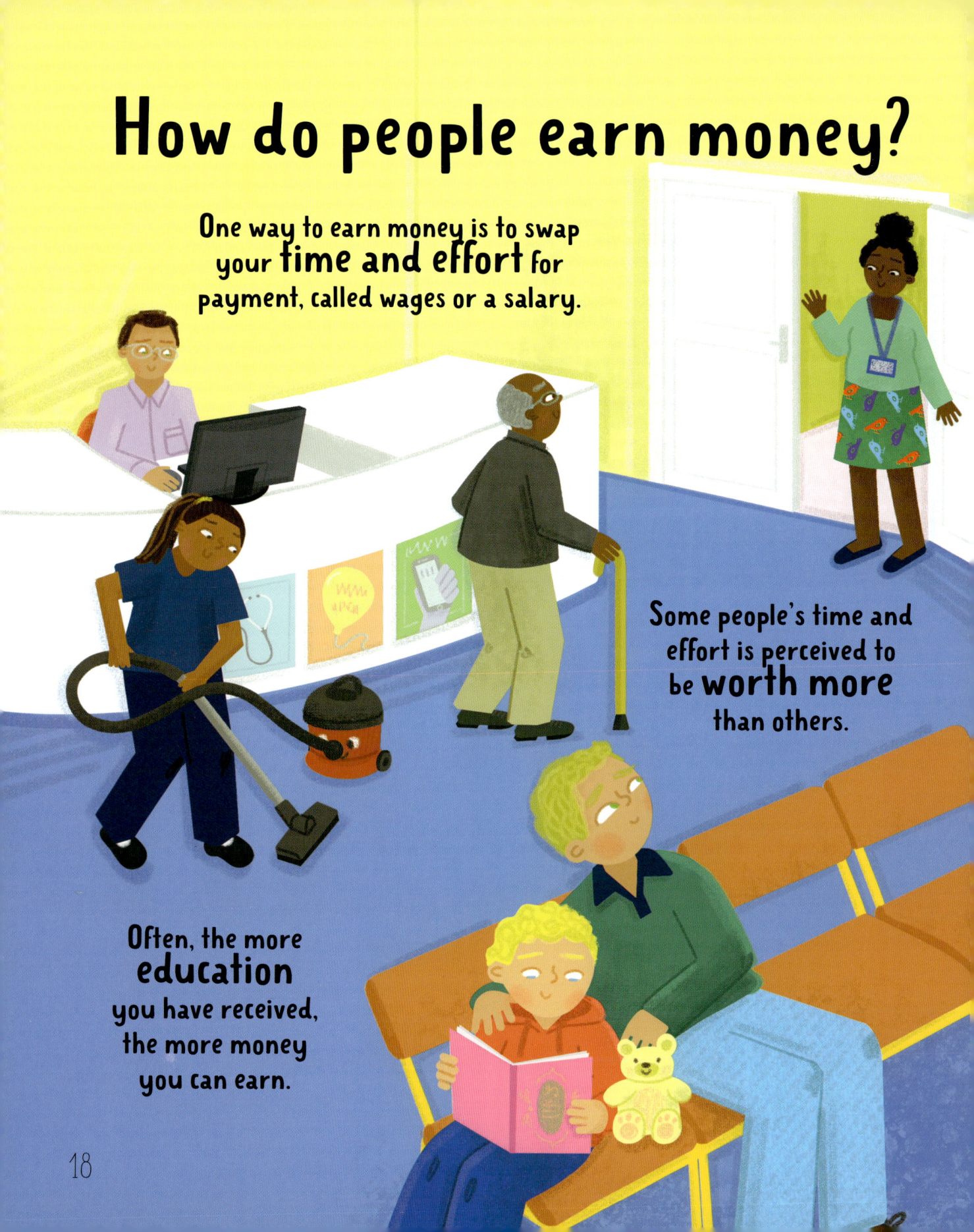

18

Another way is to make things that other people will **pay** for. Food, jewellery and art can all be created by individuals and sold to earn money.

Or you can **perform** something that people will pay to go and see, such as a song or play.

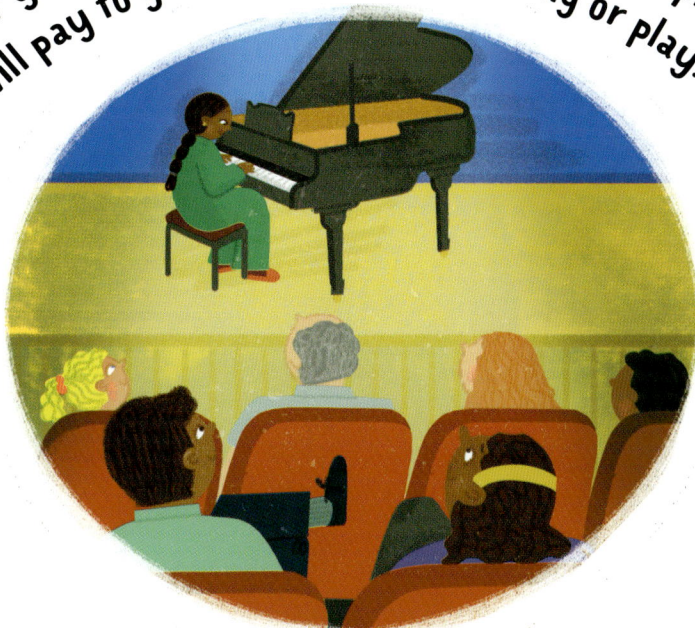

What are taxes?

Taxes are the way that a government RAISES MONEY from the people of that country to pay for things such as education, roads, refuse collection and healthcare.

There are three main areas of taxation.

Income tax is where people pay a **proportion** of what they earn to the government. This amount often increases the more someone earns.

Property taxes raise lots of money for the government. Each time a property is **sold**, the government takes its share.

The government also charges a proportion of the price of **goods and services**, such as petrol or clothing. In some countries, certain goods such as food and books are **taxfree**.

Who studies money?

Accountants study and track financial information for businesses and some individuals. They provide **reports** that help people make decisions on what to spend or save.

Tax advisors focus on making sure that people pay the right amount. Tax laws can be complicated and people can get into trouble if they don't pay the **correct sum**.

Financial advisors work with people to help them make the most of the money they have. Some help people who have run out of money and are in **debt**.

DEBT
HELP

Economists work on a larger scale to study how a **society**, such as a country or local area, manages their money.

What problems can money cause?

NOT having enough money can affect people quite severely.

Their **physical health** can suffer by not being able to buy enough food and clothing. They might not be able to afford to heat their homes.

Worrying about not being able to pay the bills can lead to **mental stress**, which in turn can make someone ill.

Obsessing about money and wanting MORE than you have can lead to destructive behaviour.

This **greed** can lead people into making poor decisions.

People can sometimes become **jealous** of others who have bigger houses, or nicer cars.

They might end up stealing the objects they think they **deserve**, like cars or smartphones.

Other people could be led astray by people who want them to do something **illegal**, such as taking bribes.

'Money is the root of all evil' is often misquoted. In fact, it should say 'the LOVE of money is the root of all evil.' It's not money itself that causes problems, just what humans do with it!

What is the future of money?

Physical money could **disappear**. The paper bills and coins that have existed for over **5000** years will no longer be used to pay for things.

Mobile pay and digital shopping will increase. There are already shops you can walk in to, put goods in your bag and leave **without paying** a cashier.

Technology registers what you've chosen and takes payment from your bank account **automatically**.

The number of different **currencies** could increase. Cryptocurrencies can be unstable so people will need to be careful.

Universal basic income is being **trialled** in a number of different countries.

This is when everyone of working age is allowed a **basic income** from the government whether they work or not.

This means people will have money to spend on what they need, which keeps the **economy** moving.

So ... do we know what money is?

Money allows us to buy what we need.
It also makes the world go around.

We know who invented money.

We understand what it is used for and how to EARN it.

We know that money is DIFFERENT all over the world.

We know who LOOKS AFTER our money.

We know we should PAY our taxes and how to make money grow.

We know that physical money is likely to disappear..

But we also understand that the GOOD that money can do, and the problems it can cause are really about people's ATTITUDES towards it.

If we want to make the world a better place, we need to understand how to make money work harder for everyone.

hats and bags

PHARMACY

BOOK

Why don't you think about what you would like to do with your money in the future?

Glossary

Accountant — a person professionally trained in accounting

Advisor — a person who gives advice and recommendations

Ancient world — the period 3000BCE-500CE

Attitude — how you feel or think about something

Barter — to trade something for something else without using money

Benefit — to do good for something or someone

Budget — the money available to use, a plan for using money

Building society — similar to a bank, it pays interest on savings and lends money for houses

Bulk — a large volume or mass

Complicated — difficult to understand or explain

Cryptocurrency — a digital currency where records are kept safe by cryptography or codes

Croesus — the King of Lydia from 585BCE-546BCE

Culture — human's intellectual accomplishments such as literature or history

Debt — when a person owes money to someone else

Destructive — intending to hurt or destroy

Digital — electronic and computer-based technology

Economist — a person who studies the economy

Economy — the organised system of money in a society

Exchange rate — the value of one currency in relation to another

Financial — the system that includes the circulation of money, banks and investments

Goods — something that has been made

Government — the institution in charge of running the country

Haggling — to argue over price

I.O.U. note — a document used to acknowledge a debt

Illegal — against the law

Income	money that is earned by working, a business or renting out property	**Proportion**	a share of something
Influence	to affect someone's behaviour	**Services**	tasks performed for the benefit of the people who request them such as window-cleaning
Interest rate	the amount paid or charged on money expressed as a percentage of the whole	**Society**	a community of people defined by common values
Invest	to put in money in order to earn a profit	**Technology**	using science to solve problems
Jealousy	to feel envy and resentment towards someone else	**The arts**	a phrase used to represent art, music and theatre
Mint	a place where coins are made	**Trade**	to swap one thing for another
Misquote	to quote wrongly	**Transfer**	to move money from one account to another
Mobile pay	payment made with a mobile phone	**Trial**	the period of time to test something new
National	owned by a nation	**Universal basic income**	where all citizens of a given group regularly receive an equal financial grant
Negotiate	to discuss something with another to reach an agreement		
Obsess	to focus entirely on something	**Value**	the amount of money something is worth
Perceive	to see	**Wealthy**	to be rich, and have lots of money
Philanthropist	someone who donates money to charity and good works		
Politician	a person who works in government